Body, Mind and You

Kotra Siva Rama Krishna

Published by Kotra Siva Rama Krishna, 2024.

While every precaution has been taken in the preparation of this book, the publisher assumes no responsibility for errors or omissions, or for damages resulting from the use of the information contained herein.

BODY, MIND AND YOU

First edition. January 15, 2024.

Copyright © 2024 Kotra Siva Rama Krishna.

ISBN: 979-8224921638

Written by Kotra Siva Rama Krishna.

Also by Kotra Siva Rama Krishna

Two Strangers On The Bed
A Girl's Conflict
Enna
Strawberry
Dusk
Just Relax!
Delicious Predicament
Nirupama
Half Opened Doors
Lovenest
Moonshine
Scarecrow
Closed Doors
Disturbed
Handfuls of Sand
Mansion of Illusions
Rain Flower
Rose Garden
Sand Dunes
Snow Flower
Split Personality
Being Possessed
Objection Sustained
House of Delusions
Rustle in the Leaves

Sasikala
Amaswitha
English Grammar Simplifier
Wisps of Smoke
Shadow in the Mirror
Love is Dangerous with a Stranger
Shadow of a Spirit
Unwanted Guests
Broken Window
Loud Thunder Nearby
Spirit in the Mirror
Whispers in the Night
Shadows in the Twilight
Twisted Shadow
Body, Mind and You
Summer Holidays
Flower of the Mist
Nail Polish
Laughter of a Spirit
Lipstick

Table of Contents

License

This ebook is licensed for your personal enjoyment only. This ebook may not be re-sold or given away to other people. If you would like to share this ebook with another person, please ask them to purchase an additional copy for each recipient. If you're reading this ebook and did not purchase it, or it was not purchased for your enjoyment only, then please return to the publisher or your favorite retailer and purchase your own copy. Thank you for respecting the hard work of this author.

About the Author

Kotra Siva Rama Krishna is an Indian English writer who is famous for his romantic, psychological thrillers. He is one of those writers who do believe that sex is one of the most important things in human beings lives. He does not want to titillate the reader but wherever there are matters related to sex, they are absolute and complete. His books are not porn but he will be open when it comes to sex in his books. He has written two non-fiction books also and they are English Grammar Simplifier and Body, Mind and You. All his books are available as ebooks and paperbacks and can be found by searching with the name 'Kotra Siva Rama Krishna'

The most surprising thing in the entire universe is the mind itself

If we encounter a little physical disturbance we immediately go to a doctor to find out a solution. But why we don't bother that much while we are suffering psychologically? Now how many people are suffering with depression, suicidal tendencies, schizophrenias and other mental illnesses? Most of them prefer to suffer like that rather than going to a psychiatrist. Very few of them do go to a psychiatrist or psychologist and find solution to their problems. Why it is so? The main reason for this is lack of awareness. It should not be forgotten that the mind is the most important component. If the mind is in good condition, very difficult tasks also can be accomplished easily. So the need of the hour is to spread the necessity about taking care of the mind particularly when it is depressed.

We have to concentrate more on our mental health rather than our physical health too. In fact our body health depends mostly on the mind. If our mind is in good condition our physical health also shall be good. If we are physically alright it contributes to our mental health. It is not so that if we are mentally alright that we shall be physically also alright and if we are physically alright that we shall be mentally also alright. Physical and mental problems may arise even one of them is perfectly alright. But body and mind contributes to each other's well being.

The most important thing in the entire universe is the mind itself. Because whatever we may do the thing that behind it is the mind itself. Behind great dams, buildings, inventions, creations and paintings, it is the mind that plays the major role. But do you know the most surprising thing here? It is the mind which is most neglected.

Whenever you disturbed a little with your body you take some reliever. If the disturbance is more you go to a physician. There are so many physicians and specialists to treat our body. There are so many medicines also available for the treatment of the same.

But how many psychiatrists and psychologists are available to treat the mind comparing with other physicians and specialists to treat the body? Even more pathetic thing is, most of the people don't even know that they are suffering psychologically and they need to consult a psychologist or psychiatrist. In most other people' opinion there is no necessity to worry about psychological ailments.

The point that needs to be etched in our minds is mind is the most important thing and it should not be neglected at all. In fact more care needs to be taken with respect to the mind comparing with the care that we are taking with respect to our body. If a healthy mind has become a sick mind it may cause lot of damage to the society to that person and to the family of that person also.

Some people cannot know that they are suffering psychologically. The people who are intimate with them has to find out the same and take them to a psychologist or psychiatrist. It has to be seen that the people should not be subjected depression. If some person appears to be depressed immediate care needs to be taken to see that he comes out of his depression.

There is more and more need of psychologists and psychiatrists. Even more need of the hour is to spread the word of importance of taking care of the mind

Only you can be the best psychologist and therapist for yourself

I don't recommend you to go to a psychologist for each and every psychological problem. Who can know more better your mind than yourself? Who can know more better than yourself from what you are mentally suffering? Then who can treat you better, give you peace than yourself? Only you can be the best psychologist and therapist for yourself. It may not be convenient to go to a psychologist even for small and minor psychological problems also. But by understanding your mind, understanding your nature, you can sort yourself most of your psychological problems.

First consider yourself as a separate person. Try to find out the solution with an openness of mind. Assess it with an impartiality. Just try to find out whether you are trying to hide anything. Try to see the roots of the problem why it has started in you at all. Then think about the solution to get rid of it.

For example you are suffering from obsessive disorder. You clean your hands many a time, see the same thing again and again. How to get rid of this obsessive disorder? Then try to know when the very first time the problem started. Were you suffering from it from your very childhood itself? Or did it start at some stage later on in your life? If you lived some of your life without suffering from this problem, it is surely possible to live the rest of your life without this problem. What all necessary is a strong resolve in yourself, perseverance and tenacity to get rid of this problem.

Imagine therapy surely shall be quite helpful in this regard. Just imagine yourself in the perfect way you want yourself to be. Do it many a time a day, not just one or two times. This gives you lot of confidence in you, slowly and slowly you can be the person you want to be.

It may appear difficult, it may appear not possible, but sure it is not so. Once you identify the gross root of your problem, it can become easier to understand it. Once you understood the problem, it can be easier to get rid of the same. As I said in the beginning of this article, only you yourself can be your best psychologist and therapist.

One caution here. All the psychological problems are not this easily possible. If they are appearing serious and persisting, consulting a professional psychologist is a must.

Mind is like a pestering child: We have to learn how to manage with it.

Ever you spend your time with children aged below eight years so? Walk with them in the streets where all types of things were available for sale? So, you sure do have an experience how the child behaves. If you are a mild and smooth character, you would be pestered to buy everything that attracts the eye of the child and almost everything attracts the eye of the child. In such situations what is the best way to behave with the children? Getting angry or beating the children does not help much. Just try to remember how you behaved in such situations. Just remain silent without bothering with the persistent demands of the child. However much the clamor of the child, don't be yielded to the demands of it. After sometime the child understands that there would be no use in pestering you and remain silent.

This is the way you need to behave with your mind also. Mind is nothing but like a pestering child. It makes all types of unnecessary demands without bothering with what type of work you are indulged in. Just don't try to reason with it or get angry or try to come terms with it. Just be calm without bothering whatever may be it demands. After sometime it very well understands that there is no use in pestering you with demands and remain silent.

You just need to learn how to go along with the mind and manage it. I don't use the word discipline here. It is too harsh a word and you cannot discipline your mind. If you try to discipline, if you try to put your mind into order, it becomes even more wild. Just learn how to manage with it and how to go along with it.

The three states of mind: you need to keep a watch on it

When I said three states of mind, I don't mean waking state, dreaming state and deep sleep state. These three states are different and they relates to thinking. Sometimes thoughts come all by themselves into your mind which is unintentional thinking. Sometimes you particularly think about something and it is intentional thinking. Sometimes there would be no thoughts either intentional or unintentional, the mind remains blank and it is a neutral stage.

In whatever state your mind may be you have to keep a watch on it. You need not make air tight concentration on your mind and see what it is doing. If you try to do it like that it gets you headache. Just try to be conscious what your mind is doing. Even sometimes you slip watching the mind there is no problem whatsoever. Put yourself on the job again keeping a smile on your lips. If you do it relaxingly it is fun and very soon you start enjoying it because it gives you a feeling that you are distinct and different from your mind.

The problem comes in differentiating between the intentional and unintentional thoughts. Even the mind put the thoughts without your intention, you think you are doing the thoughts intentionally. If you go on with practicing, you can know whether you are thinking intentionally or thoughts come all by themselves.

The whole thing lies in a simple technique: Systematically separate yourself form the mind

Yes. If you understand, if you try to do just as I have said you sure can understand the substance in my saying. All the time you are separate, distinct and different from the mind. Just because you are associating yourself with the mind, thinking yourself that you are the mind, causing the whole set of problems. It may be difficult to think that you are different from the mind. You just cannot imagine yourself how you are different from the mind. But I can show you and demonstrate to you how and why you are not the mind and different from the mind.

Before going into the matter how you are not the mind and different from it, we shall see what exactly this mind is. You may have heard many a time that the mind is nothing but bundle of thoughts (imaginations, visualizations and feelings collectively take as thoughts). That means there is no mind if there are no thoughts. These thoughts are like clouds in the sky and they come and go and you can see the thoughts and know about the thoughts. If we take that you are the mind itself (then thoughts itself) who it is observing the thoughts? This itself clearly demonstrates that you are different from the thoughts

I shall give you another example to demonstrate to you that you are not the mind. Ever you find yourself suddenly thinking about something without your knowledge at all? You may be doing something like walking, reading, writing, etc. and your mind go on thinking about something without your knowledge at all. With a jerk in the middle of whatever you may be doing it is either reading or writing or something else, you find yourself thinking about something without your knowledge.

The surprising thing to be noticed here is, while you have engaged yourself in something wholeheartedly then what it is engaged in some other thinking? This is the simple example and demonstration to say that you are not the mind but different from the mind. If you are the mind itself then there is no chance that you go from the task you put yourself in wholeheartedly to think something entirely different.

Then I venture to ask you to think about deep sleep. Where are these thoughts then? Absolutely nowhere. Do you say that you are not in existence at all as there are no thoughts in deep sleep? No. Then what is in existence while you are in deep sleep? It is pure 'you' but nothing else. The pure 'you' shall be like that. The deep sleep is a gift to us from God to understand our real selves.

Just think about deep sleep. As many people think, deep sleep is not at all an inactive or lethargy state. It is not all a nil state or state of nothing. It is a state which is most potential and useful to us. Just try to remember how do you feel in deep sleep? You just want to be in it all the time, forever and infinite. If someone disturbed you while you are sleeping deeply, you get angry and you become annoyed. Why so? Because it is a blissful state and it is a state of you which you don't want to leave at all. Therefore, it is that much dearer and that much sweeter to you.

In fact that state you are in while you fall into deep sleep is not something you have to get. Because when you get rid of mind (the thoughts) that is what remains. It is just like the screen in a movie theatre. When there are movies projecting on the screen, you do see only the pictures. When the pictures stopped only the screen remains. In the same way when the thoughts are going on (mind is in existence) you do see only the thoughts. But when the thoughts stop (mind ceases to exist), you remain and you came into the experience of yourself.

The only problem here is you yourself are not able to stop the thoughts. They have to be stopped themselves as they are in the deep sleep. If we allow it to be so we get that blissful stage only in our deep sleep. The main thing to consider here is how to stop the thoughts. I am going to tell you about how to stop thoughts in my next article.

How to stop thoughts?

You can say this in another way how to make the mind non-existing as the mind is nothing but a bundle of thoughts. Can we do that willfully or intentionally? Can we stop the thoughts coming into our mind? Can we make the mind non-existing at will?

Try to follow whatever your method you have heard or coming to know to stop the thoughts and see that the thoughts are giving a pause or not. I agree that sure there shall be a pause in the thoughts but it would not be much. Moreover it is not going to be comfortable for you. In that forceful thought-less stage you cannot feel the bliss which you do feel in your deep sleep. My sincere suggestion to you is don't try to stop the thoughts at will. Don't try to make the mind nil at force.

Alright then, what should be done? Should you remain a victim of thoughts all the time? Is there no way at all to enjoy the bliss which we enjoy in our deep sleep in any other time? Sure there is. I am going to clarify this for you.

What you need to understand at the first place is thoughts or the mind you may apply whichever term you feel more comfortable to you is not at all dangerous or harmful. It is not the thoughts that are bothering you but it is your feelings created by those thoughts that bother you. First of all you have to understand the incessant nature of the mind or thoughts. If they do come, just let them come all the time, what is the problem? Let all types of thoughts fill your mind you just don't bother. After waking up you hear many types of sounds around you till you fall asleep in the night, would you bother at all? Consider the unnecessary or unintentional thoughts in the same way. Don't even acknowledge those thoughts and just let them take a whirlwind tour of your mind.

It may appear difficult and frustrating in the beginning. But if you do go practicing it, it becomes quite easier to you. The surprising thing here is once you start disregarding the unnecessary thoughts they automatically stop bothering you. Gradually you yourself can witness a calm and peaceful state in yourself.

The most important thing that needs to be noticed here is, once you have excelled in practicing this technique, even there are all sorts of unintentional or involuntary thoughts in you, they don't bother you at all. You can feel as much comfortable and peaceful as possible even with all these noisy unnecessary thoughts as you do feel while none of these thoughts are present, once you have become an expert in disregarding the unnecessary thoughts

Positive thinking and negative thinking

The advocates of positive thinking do say to fill our mind always with positive thoughts. They are all quite against with negative thinking. In their saying, whenever we find ourselves thinking about something negative we have to replace it immediately with some positive thinking. Because in their opinion positive thinking gets us positive results and negative thinking gets us negative results. Particularly the advocates for law of attraction urge us to keep our mind only with positive thinking all the time.

Before delve myself into the point whether particular way of thinking gets us particular results or not, I simply ask is it is possible to replace a negative thought with a positive thought as soon as it comes into our mind? For example you are doing something seriously in your office and some negative thought trespassed into your mind. Can you stop whatever you are doing immediately and bother yourself to replace that negative thought with some positive thought? Even you want to do it like that another problem immediately comes to you is with which positive thought you have to replace that negative thought. Even you do pull all your strength and do it like that, for how many negative thoughts you can do it so?

I cannot say whether keeping your mind all the time with positive thoughts gets you positive results or not but if you try to replace your negative thoughts with positive thoughts all the time it creates an intensive inner conflict. You start feeling headache and your positive thinking does not give you relaxation or peace.

Don't think I am in favour of negative thinking and against positive thinking. I am just trying to say that you should try to understand your mind and go along with it. At the same time what I want to say is, basing on my personal experience so far till now, till this very moment of writing this article, outside happenings have nothing to do with your inside thinking.

Even you fill your mind with the thinking that you have become a very rich man in the world for one week continuously it does not get even a hundred rupees note or one dollar. In the same way even you felt fear that you have become afflicted with a dangerous disease continuously, nothing like that happens.

The outside things are having their own way to happen and they don't bother to see into your mind to know what you are thinking and then happen. I repeat, they have their own way to happen. So, don't worry if negative thoughts are persistently coming into your mind because they cannot do any harm to you. Just leave the thoughts on their own way whether they are negative or positive without analyzing them.

Even the thinking does not affect the outside happenings, thinking positive is good and try to keep your mind with good thoughts whenever you can. But don't force yourself to think positively all the time at the risk of your relaxation. At the same time don't feel fear to negative thoughts and don't try to force them out of your mind with all your might as soon as they enter into your mind. If the negative thoughts are persistent, let them linger in your mind as long as they do want. Once the negative thoughts understand you just don't care about them at all, they just disappear and left you in peace.

The incongruities I found in the sayings of the preachers of 'Law of Attraction.'

I am not against law of attraction. It may work if it has been practiced in the way as per the sayings of the well experienced practitioners. But I found a difficulty in understanding the two principles the great teachers of 'law of attraction' all the time saying.

First principle: "your subconscious does not know the difference between reality and imagination. If you impress on it something false or something dangerous, it executes the same without showing any discretion. So, be careful in what you are impressing on your subconscious."

Second principle: "your subconscious mind is omnipotent and there is nothing difficult to it to do. It need not have taken time either. What all you need to do is just pray it to do something and you get it. What all you need to do is to put absolute trust in the subconscious."

They call this 'subconscious' with various names, infinite intelligence, creative intelligence, universal intelligence, like that. In their opinion this subconscious is equal to god and it is there just to fulfill all our wishes if they have been asked in the way they ought to be asked.

The problem here is, if this subconscious mind is something like god, omnipotent why can't it differentiate between reality and imagination? Is something god like thing has handicaps like these? How it goes to execute something blindly just by getting impression on it without bothering whether it is good or not to do so?

The other thing that bothers me is 'absolute trust.' How we can put our absolute faith on something without having any experience with it?

You trust your friend because you know him for a long time and he helped you many a time and stood with you in your difficulties. You trust your typing capacity because you are having wonderful experience while typing. In this way to trust something we must have some experience with it. Without having any experience like this, I just cannot understand how we can put absolute trust on the subconscious.

I am reiterating once again that I am not against 'Law of Attraction'. If it works as it has been said by the practitioners of it, I and many other people do feel so happy. But these are points that are troubling me.

How to change negative thinking into positive thinking?

This is not going to be possible at once. Moreover if you tend to think negatively from scratch, it becomes some more difficult. But the point hereto noticeable is it is not impossible. Just try to see before you start thinking positively why and how you tend to think only negatively? Look into your past, mostly into your childhood. The way you have been treated and programmed in your childhood plays a major role when you became an adult. It is mostly the parents who first program their children minds. If they first tell their children that they cannot do anything, they are fools, anyone else is better than them it shall be etched strongly on their minds. Therefore it is very important not to program negatively while you are talking with your children.

Alright, the present task now. First affirm yourself that your negative way of thinking is only because of the wrong programming or something external reason but not natural at all. Then start thinking positively about those things which you think particularly negatively. For example if you visualize your office environment as something troublesome, problem creating, start visualizing it as something that gives you ample opportunity to prove yourself. If you always imagine your wife as someone creates pain for something or other, start imaging her as helping and cheerful companion always. This positive thinking sure appears difficult in the beginning. But if you continue practicing soon you can see the change.

One important point. Don't use force for thinking positively. At the same time there is no necessity to feel fear for negative thinking.

Just relaxingly and cheerfully try to replace the negative thinking with positive thinking and positive thinking sure would be quite helpful to you. It fills your heart with happiness. You can do your work more heartily and happily with postitive thinking inside.

Only feelings do matter

Most people think thoughts plays an important role in our minds. In fact it is not so. It is the feelings that do play a very important role. Most of the thoughts do create feelings either happy or sorrow depend upon the nature of the thoughts. At the same time, there is no necessity that each and every thought does create a feeling. A thought about next elections may not evoke any feeling in you. The thought regarding the praise by your boss on yesterday evening does create a good feeling. The thought regarding the quarrel between you and your wife two days back creates a sad feeling. Thoughts that do not create either happiness or sorrow are called as neutral thoughts. At the same time, there is no necessity that every feeling should be evoked by a thought. Feelings can be there without preceding by a thought. A month aged baby cannot have any thoughts. But it sure does have feelings. A crying baby stops that and smile happily when its mother took it into her hands.

But the point is, if you can control the thoughts, you can control the feelings. If you do see that only good thoughts come into your mind all the time, you do get only good feelings. By cultivating only good feelings you can change your whole life. It is a hard exercise in fact but it is also possible with constant practice.

Is self hypnotism beneficial?

Sure it is. Self hypnotism is quite beneficial if it has been understood in a right perspective. It should not be understood as something with which we can do anything. We can get rid of bad habits, develop confidence, remove mental blocks, better our concentration skills, etc. with the help of self hypnotism. First of all we have to understand what is self-hypnotism. Then it shall be possible to us to practice it.

Self hypnotism helps in programming our sub-conscious mind while we are in alpha state of mind. One more thing we need to understand here is the alpha state of mind. In alpha state of mind thoughts would be reduced to minimum. Conscious mind would be in a very relaxed state and about to fall asleep. Whatever you may say to yourself in that state would sink easily into your subconscious mind. If you want to quit smoking, you can program yourself accordingly in that alpha state of mind.

You have to put yourself in that alpha state of mind to program yourself with self-hypnotism. When you are in that alpha state of mind you have to give yourself the suggestions like 'from now on I am free from this habit of smoking.' It may not give you the best result in the first session itself. To have the complete impact of it you need to practice it number of times. But it sure does give the desired result if you do it regularly for some days.

Now we shall see how to put ourselves into alpha state of mind. Make yourself completely comfortable in a chair. The chair must be so that there should be no uncomfortability to your back. Close your eyes and take three or four deep breaths. Deep breathing automatically relaxes you completely. Then start counting numbers. No haste.... No fast... Just say one, two, three .... After counting some twenty or so, you stop counting and find yourself in a calm and peaceful state. You can call this state as alpha state of mind.

If sitting in a chair does not work for you, you may try this in lying position on the bed also. The only thing you need to be quite careful is not to fall asleep. If you practice regularly, you can very easily put yourself into alpha state of mind in quite less time.

What is imaginal therapy? Is it is useful to us?

Imaginal therapy means imagining ourselves that we are free from a particular disease, habit, etc. Suppose someone is suffering from smoking habit. He has to imagine himself minimum five minutes everyday that he is completely free of that habit. Not immediately but slowly it starts giving result. One can develop self-confidence to get rid of bad habits in this way. This imaginal therapy can be used for certain type of deceases also. One thing must be remember quite clear here. It is not at all a complete substitution for medication or treatment. Someone imagining himself as a healthy man while suffering from some decease surely be helpful to him and make him good in less time. But he must not stop the usual medication and treatment.

How to deal with thoughts?

Before we know or discuss about how to deal with thoughts, it is important that we know the type of thoughts. Thoughts are two types. Intentional thoughts and unintentional thoughts. Intentional thoughts are those which you do intentionally. You shall have control over the intentional thoughts. There is no necessity to worry much about these intentional thoughts. The next are unintentional thoughts. These unintentional thoughts do come all the time. You need not do them at all. Whatever you may be doing, they just pop-up into you. These unintentional thoughts consist pleasant and unpleasant thoughts also.

The main problem is, whenever thoughts unintentionally pop-up into you, you think that you are doing those thoughts intentionally. Then you become irritated. You are doing something important and want to do with all the concentration but these unintentional thoughts trouble you coming from nowhere. Sometimes you stop and try to clear these unintentional thoughts but they do become even more and their strength would become even more. Whenever you try to clear the unintentional thoughts and remove them from your mind, it happens like this. Then what we should do?

Here the solution. Just don't bother about these unintentional thoughts. Gently remind yourself that you have no business with these unintentional thoughts. Treat these unintentional thoughts just like you treat the outside disturbances. Once you stop worrying about these unintentional thoughts and stop fighting with them, they do weaken. Either they do become disappear or even they are there, they don't bother you anymore.

Sometimes there may be some useful tips in these unintentional thoughts. So, don't try to run away from the unintentional thoughts and whenever you find some useful thought in these unintentional thoughts note it somewhere.

It is not going to be possible just in one day or one week to learn to deal with unintentional thoughts in this way. At the same time it is very difficult to find the difference between intentional and unintentional thoughts. But practice wins every time. If you are persistent you sure do get control over unintentional thoughts.

Managing life

Just plan this day. Don't worry about yesterday. Don't think about tomorrow. Live on this day. As fully as possible. Don't try to do the work you are doing in a routine or mechanical way. It is important to enjoy whatever we are doing. How menial, how low, even you are doing the work under compulsion, just try to enjoy it.

Never think menial about work. Never develop hate towards work. Work is like food to your mind and it is as much necessary to your mind as food is necessary to your body. Just try to remain a single day without doing any work at all. By the end of the day you almost become mad. You just crave for doing something. In fact if you have been deprived of all work and made to sit idle, you do crave for it more than you do crave for anything else.

We all do like to do the work we like. But all of us cannot get the work we like to do. Sometimes we do feel very much burdensome or irritated at what we are doing since it is not something we can enjoy. In such situations just try to like what you are doing. If you cannot do what you enjoy then you try to enjoy what you are doing. It is easier said than doing but not impossible. It sure gives you joy and a sense of commitment and fulfillment. Your confidence shall be tremendously boosted. If you try this you sure come to know the truth in what I have said.

Proposing mind and analyzing mind

Our mind can be divided into two types. Proposing mind and analyzing mind. The proposing mind would make one or the other proposal all the time. It never stops. It never gets fatigue. The analyzing mind would take the points the proposing mind makes and try to analyze them. Whether it is useful or not, even it is disgusting, the analyzing mind takes the points the proposing mind makes and try to analyze them. In that process it sometimes feels happy. Sometimes feel sorrow. Sometimes gets irritation and anger. The analyzing mind just becomes a slave in the hands of the proposing mind.

You cannot stop the proposing mind. You just cannot control it and it throws one or other thought all the time. But you can stop the analyzing mind. You just can remain calm without bothering about the proposals made by the proposing mind. Once you remain without being influenced by the proposing mind its force on you becomes weakened. No surprise after some days it stops proposing unnecessary thoughts to you.

Next time when you do get unnecessary thoughts into your mind, don't dwell on them. Just remind yourself that they are the propositions made by the proposing mind and you can remain without analyzing them. Just see what a change you can get in yourself!

Is there a thinker or there are only thoughts?

It may be some valued thinkers opinion that there is no thinker but only thoughts but I cannot fully agree with it. If there is no thinker whatsoever at all, who is saying 'I am having this thought.' Who is thinking 'I don't like this thought, I have to change it.' Who is being influenced by these thoughts and becoming sad or happy? So undoubtedly there is someone who is observing the thoughts, who is being influenced by thoughts and sometimes he wanted to change those thoughts also.

In my opinion thoughts are like circles on a lake and tides in an ocean. In fact circles on a lake are not different from the lake. They are part of the lake itself. In the same way tides are not different from the ocean. They are the part of the ocean. In the same way thoughts are also not different from you but they are part of you. There can be a lake without circles but circles cannot happen without a lake. There can be an ocean without tides but tides cannot be in existence without ocean. In the same way there can be you without thoughts but thoughts cannot be in existence without you.

Yes. You can be there without thoughts in a peaceful, calm and blissful way. Deep sleep is the perfect testimonial to this. Where are these thoughts while you are in deep sleep? But still you are in existence in deep sleep too. How nice and how good the state in deep sleep is! How much we crave ourselves to be in such a state always!

Why do we feel fear to keep our minds thought free?

It is of course difficult to keep the mind thought free. Even it is possible, at the first place, most of us don't like to keep the mind thought free. We just don't like it. If we have got a sign that our mind has become empty, we immediately pull one or other thoughts into it. If you don't believe me, you just observe yourself and see. Though many a time you say that thoughts are torturing you and you want to get rid of them, you don't like a mind without thoughts. (In fact there is no mind without thoughts). You sure do pull some thought, even it causes unpleasantness to you into your mind rather than leaving it empty.

It is so because you think you are the thoughts and you are the mind. In your opinion there is no existence to you, no identity to you at all without thoughts. What I am if there is no mind? You think. The possible answer appalls you. Therefore all the time you bother yourself to keep your mind with one thought or the other.

This is not true at all. The true existence of you comes into light only when all the thoughts cease. The solemnity and the peace that would be evident in that silence would be great. Yes, it is a little fearsome to the beginner, to the amateur, to the inexperienced. But it is not so to the person who knew about it and experienced it. Such state very occasionally occurs and when it happens don't wish it to go away and don't try to pull any thought into your mind even very nobler one either. Just observe the calm and peaceful state however long it goes like that.

What is meditation? When we can practice it?

Without knowing what is meditation that thing may not give you much benefit. Now a day this term has gained a lot of popularity and everyone practicing it (Atleast they are thinking that they are practicing it). There are many ways and many methods to practice meditation. Numerous institutions and websites came into birth to teach about meditation.

The name of it itself to some extent tell us what is meditation. It means 'think about something' or 'cogitate about something'. But to think about what? Cogitate about what? About yourself, about what exactly you are.

Rather than considering it in its literal meaning, we do take it as 'relaxing.' Relaxing ourselves from the troubling mind or making ourselves free from the troubling mind. Some people do say we have to sit straight and concentrate on Christ centre (the centre place between the two eye brows), some people do say we have to say a name repeatedly. Some other people say we have to start analyzing what the "I" feeling is. There are some more ways to practice meditation.

Yes, all these ways are true and correct. They help you to give the fruit of meditation to some extent but not completely. The main draw back in using the above methods is you have to put your mind into some exercise. You have to force it to do something. Mind is like a recalcitrant child and it does not want to be focused on anything. If you do try to put it on something with force, it violates and retaliates. It is just like disciplining an imbecile child.

Mind always wants to be scattered and spread rather than pointed. The experience we do have in making it pointed for whatever may be the purpose not going to be very pleasant. The relaxation we do have (If we do take the meditation as extreme relaxation) by following the above methods or some other methods would not be much, moreover there may be pains, headache and tension also result from that.

Then what is the best way to practice meditation? Just let the mind go in its way. You need not even observe what you are doing. At the same time there is no problem if the minds vagaries came into your notice. Just leave it on its own and remain yourself. Just remind yourself strongly that you are not the mind and mind following its nature. It may be appeared absurd in the beginning but if you go on practicing it you can know the sweetness in it. You can feel such relaxation which you cannot feel in any other way at all.

The other point needs to be considered is, when and how it should be practiced? Is there a particular posture we need to take while practicing this meditation? Not at all. There is no particular posture you need to take while practicing this meditation. You may practice it at any time you want. You just do whatever you are doing, putting as much focus as it needs while leaving the mind on its own.

Sure all the thoughts and vagaries of your mind come into your notice but you don't effect by them at all. You can see your mind completely separate from you just like a companion working with you then. It would be fun and you sure can enjoy it.

What causes depression?

Now a day we are hearing a lot about this depression. It is important to know about it and the steps we have to take to cure it. Depression is a term that relates to the mind and psychology. Depression means feeling terribly bad or becoming horribly inferior. Generally tension and worry do cause the depression and heavy work pressure either in home or in office or in other places also causes this depression. Continuous failures in doing something or not getting success even after trying for something many a time also causes this depression.

We can notice the people suffering from depression with a little observation. They don't talk much and they want to be secluded from others. They get easily irritated and annoyed. The main problem is they cannot themselves know that they are suffering from depression and that needs to be treated.

If you find these symptoms in your relatives or friends the first thing you need to do is don't get angry with them when they irritate on you or try to escape from you. It is better try to know whether they are suffering from any failures or have not got something after vigorous trying or feeling pressure for anything. Despite their being trying to avoid you in all the ways possible, you must try to join them and try to talk with them. It is important that you have to let them know that they are suffering from depression and that needs to be treated otherwise it shall have serious consequences. You need to do it very patiently making them understand it without letting them become even more inferior or even more worried.

It may not be someone else, you yourself sometimes be a target to this depression. It is easier to treat yourself rather than treating other people. The first and foremost thing needs to be done is to get some extreme relaxation. Every day you have to allot some time particularly for yourself and you do anything that would be quite amusing and fun to you. You may go to a movie, read something or write something or paint something or listen something whichever gives you the most pleasure. Meditation in a relaxed way also helps a lot to cure ourselves from this depression.

If this depression has not been cured by simple and small techniques, going to a psychologist or psychiatrist is must for the treatment of it.

There is time, only if you are conscious of it:

Time is a mythical thing. In fact there is no time like thing at all. It can be said that the time is more like a feeling rather than something substantial. It is abstract.

Time is there only if you do feel it or if you are conscious of it. If you don't feel or if you are not conscious there is no time at all to you. For example just try to remember how you have felt while watching a very interesting movie. A movie lasts atleast two and half hours. How you have passed those two and half hours? You did not feel the time. When the movie comes to an end you feel surprise how the two and half hours have been passed! It simply demonstrates time is just your feeling. If you disregard it there is no time at all.

I shall give you another example. Here you know how you do feel every second of the time. Just remember the last time when you have felt so excited, so fearsome and anxious. You feel every second of passage of time. A second passed like an hour to you. Here time is in existence for you.

Those people who are very happy don't feel time. They just cannot notice when their youth has passed and when they have become old. Once they become old and vegetables they too do start feeling the time.

The best way to pass time fast is stop noticing it unnecessarily. Don't worry about time now and then but put yourself wholeheartedly into something and start enjoying it. Then you just don't know the passage of time.

I have dealt with time in a limited sense but not in a broader sense. In a broader sense time is there and time is god itself. In broader sense time gets changes into things. In a wider way time creates, maintains and destroys things.

I feeling and I thought

What is the best way of meditation? Thinking about the 'I' feeling or 'I' thought in the body or disregarding it completely.

'I' is the most important feeling or thought. There is no doubt at all. But the point we have to consider here is do we need to meditate over it all the time or disregard it. As per Ramana Maharshi's saying that there is no 'I' like thing at all and it is just a thought. As there is nothing like that at all, what would be the use in thinking or worrying about it? In my opinion and in my experience disregarding this 'I' feeling or 'I' thought is the best way to get absolute peace. I can demonstrate to you how it works out like that.

Just remember the times when you have read a good book or watched a very interesting movie. What happened then? You have forgotten about everything and completely involved in the movie you were watching or the book you were reading. You were in a bliss like taste. After watching of the movie or reading of the book was completed, wearily you came into this world again. All the worldly things come into your notice again and start bothering you.

Now we shall consider what happened exactly while you were watching the movie or reading the book. What gave you that much of joy then? It is not because you have involved in something very funny or joyous but because you have forgotten or disregarded something. That something is 'I' feeling. Just because you have forgotten or disregarded that 'I' feeling, you put yourself in that much of joy. If you can forget or disregard that 'I' feeling, you can enjoy such peace or such bliss all the time. You need not particularly watch or read something funny and joyous.

Why disregarding or forgetting about the 'I' feeling does give us such happiness or joy? It is so because that there is no 'I' at all and it is just a mythical thing. If you are thinking about yourself or 'I', you are just clinging to an unimportant and non-existent thing.

Out of the body experience

You are not the body. You are different from the body. It is indeed quite strange to think like this. I do tell you an exercise through which you can get out of the body experience. It is not easy and it requires effort. But if you do practice it diligently, per severely it sure does work for you

To do this, just sit yourself in a chair and make yourself completely relaxed. The best way to make yourself instantly relaxed is to take three or four deep breaths. The chair needs to be so that your back should feel comfort.

I have to say here itself that it is not so easy an exercise. But if you persist with practice you can gain easiness. Once you start experiencing it, you do have wonderful feeling and you really enjoy it. I shall tell you now what you need to do once you comfortably settled in the chair.

It can be practiced either by closing your eyes or by opening them. Try to think about your body. With what it made of? Bones, muscles, pus, blood, etc. Whatever that may be in our body it is just made of atoms but nothing else. It is just a moss of matter. If it is scanned and x-rayed just the matter would be found and nothing else.

Then think what is the 'I' feeling in your body? Why you cannot see it? Why it cannot be found? It takes time to immerse yourself in this way of thinking. But once your mind completely involved in this thinking you do get a very strange feeling. Slowly and slowly you get a feeling that you are completely separate from your body.

Give more preference to think about the body rather than what you are in the body. Once you understood your body is nothing but moss of matter, automatically the feeling you are not the body developed more and more. In this way you can systematically separate yourself from the body.

Can we control our mind completely?

It is the biggest mistake of us to think that we can control our mind completely. However great we may become, however biggest tasks we may have accomplished, we cannot take our mind completely into our hands. It is just like the body which has its own nature and cannot get rid of it under normal circumstances. Whenever you go into sunshine and expose yourself to sunrays, it is the nature of the body to perceive the heat and convey that feeling to the mind. In the same way if some ice cubes have been put on your hand, your body shall perceive the feeling of cooling and convey it to the mind. If you sit on a rock, on a hard surface, it is the duty of your body to perceive the hardness and send that feeling to the mind.

In the same way the mind also has its own nature. If someone praises it feels good and proud. If someone criticizes it feels sad and bad. In the same way it feels envy, jealousy, anger, happiness, etc. depending on the situation it faces. You just cannot change the nature of your mind and stop it from feeling just like as you cannot stop your body from sensing.

Then what is the best thing to do here? Just remind yourself you are not the mind and jealousy, envy, anger, etc. feelings are not yours. It may appear odd in the beginning difficult to practice but if you are persistent in practicing it it sure does give you good result. Surprisingly you can get control over your mind.

Come out of your false identifications

Before coming out of false identifications it is important to know about these. You are thinking I am the body. It is a false identification. You are thinking I am the mind. It is also a false identification. You have to come out of these false identifications because these false identifications limit you. These false identifications create problems to you.

Keeping yourself in these false identifications is just like thinking yourself as a poor man when you are the richest person in the world. But how one can come out of these false identifications? Just think about the body. What it is? If it has been cut into pieces what would be found? Just blood, muscle, bones, pus, etc. Can you agree any of these can be you? No. None of these can be you. At the same time every day you are seeing so many people dying for variety of reasons. Even nothing happens on one day in future this body stops functioning. Why it stops functioning? Because something that makes it functioning all the time leaves it. That something which leaves the body is you. Not the body. Whenever you are saying I am forty two years aged or sixty two years aged, you are saying that basing on our body. In the same way, the classification of male and female also based on the body only. When you are not the body itself, how you do have any age? How you do can be male or female?

Then you think if I am not the body I may be the mind. Thinking yourself as the mind is better than thinking yourself as the body but it is also not true. Before coming to the point whether you are the mind or not, we shall see what the mind exactly is. Some philosopher said, mind is nothing but a bundle of thoughts. (Thoughts consist imaginations, visualizations and feelings also). But where are these thoughts while you are in deep sleep? As there are no thoughts while you are in deep sleep, do you say you are not in existence or dead in deep sleep? No, you are in existence while you are in deep sleep also. Therefore which is not in existence in your deep sleep are only thoughts, that is the mind. That means while you are in deep sleep the mind is not in existence. You are always in existence. By this it can be easily said that you are not the mind.

In fact it is not difficult to convince anyone that he is not the mind and he is not the body. But the question he immediately asks is, if he is not the body, if he is not the mind, what he is then? He is something that cannot be defined. He has not been made of atoms as the material world made. He does not occupy space. He is not limited to time. He is in existence all the time and everywhere he is present but it is completely impossible to define him. He is undefinable 'Achintyam' in Sanskrit

The body, mind and you

On one day a seventy years aged man went to the doctor taking his ten years grandson with him. The old man told his problems to the doctor. Doctor examined him and prescribed a battery of tests, scans and x-rays. The grandfather and grandson came out and then they went to the adjoined laboratory and the grandfather gave his blood for all those different tests and posed himself for all those scans and x-rays. The grandson observed everything keenly.

While they both were waiting for the blood tests results and other outputs, the grandson asked his grandfather "grandpa, for what about all these blood tests, scans and x-rays?"

"They do tell what is wrong with my body." looking into the inquisitive eyes of his grandson grandfather replied, "The blood tests tell us whether sugar is under control or not, how is the cholesterol condition, etc. The other scans and x-rays tell us how my bones, neurals, heart and other things."

"Whose body this is?" the grandson asked as if he did not hear any of that.

"It is mine, of course." Wondering why his grandson asked such a stupid question the grandfather said.

"Are you sure that it is your body?" the grandson persisted.

"You must have lost your mind. This is my body and it is I." looking angrily at his grandson the grandfather said.

"If you are that much assertive that it is your body," the grandson paused for a moment. "Why the hell you did come to some other person to know about what is wrong with it? If it is you, the body is you, why don't you, yourself can be known the sugar level, the cholesterol level and other positions of it?"

"I did not think about it so. I never have thought in this angle." The dumbfounded grandfather said.

Not just that grandfather, so many of us never consider this strange fact. The most surprising thing in the world is that we don't feel any surprise to those things to which we have to feel lot of surprise. Yes, it is your body, you always claim without any ambiguity it is 'you'. Then why do you have to go to someone else whenever it encounters a small problem? Why don't you know yourself what is wrong with it since it is you but nothing else? Why some doctor examines you and prescribes tests? It is all appearing nonsense, is it is not? If you don't concentrate much, if you don't think much, it appears like that.

So, please pause a while. Think. It is your body, it is you in fact, then why it is such an alien thing to you? Why don't you know how your kidneys look like? How your heart looks like? How your lungs look like? How they do work? Why your blood is red in colour?

You may say that you know answers to all these questions. But how did you come to know the answers to these questions? Not because it is you or your body. But because someone else did research on the other people bodies and came to know and told the same around the world. But not all by yourself!

By the above, it can be easily said that you are not the body. You are just identifying yourself with the body. Why this identification? Is identification is a must?

Yes. Identification with something is must as far as our mind is concerned. Our mind cannot understand that there can be something in existence without being made of atoms, without occupying space. Its comprehensive power is not that much to understand the feeling of 'I' in the body is something which is not made of atoms, which does not require space and which has no form. Mind cannot be rest in peace unless this 'I' feeling is identified with something. So that something so handy to accommodate the 'I' feeling is body itself. So in mind's opinion the body is the 'I'.

The interesting part is even the facts are available, even it can analyse and decide that the 'I' is not the body, mind does not want to do so. It just never prefers to go into that analysation since thinking 'I' as the body is comfortable and convenient. There are things that can be known which are not made of atoms, which do not occupy space. Feelings are like that. Happiness, sorrow, envy which can be known as they made their presence be known very well to us and they are not made of atoms. They do not occupy space. Thoughts are also like that. You can comprehend the presence of thoughts. They too are not made of atoms and do not occupy space. Mind can come to an opinion by this that 'I' feeling is something like that not being made of atoms and not occupying space. It just does not want to. But why? Already the reason was told. Thinking the body as 'I' is comfortable and convenient.

Taking 'I' as the body may be comfortable and convenient but not harmless. At the same time it does not remain comfortable and convenient always like that and sometimes it proves to be most inconvenient, uncomfortable. Coming out of the feeling that 'I' is the body is most important. In fact, after accomplishing it, one can feel so much of happiness, convenience and comfortability.

Before we discuss how to separate ourselves from the feeling of 'I' as body, we have to think of what is this feeling of 'I'. Once you start thinking about this feeling of 'I', it proves to be very surprising, strange and curious. By delving deep in thinking about 'I' itself makes you known 'I' is not the body.

Bhagawan Ramana Maharshi said 'I' is nothing but first and foremost thought. First this thought comes and then all the other thoughts follow it. If this 'I' is perished and destroyed by self inquiry, all the other thoughts also met with the same fate.

I am not going to contradict with what Bhagawan Ramana Maharshi said. But here is a simple problem. No thought can happen all by itself, in isolation, atleast as far as our comprehension abilities are concerned. I agree this 'I' feeling is nothing but a thought. But to whom this I feeling is happening then? Occurring then?

Why do we give ourselves that much importance to our body? Why do we feel so happy when someone praises us that we are beautiful or handsome? Moreover why do we feel fear to death, to leave the body? Is it is all just because you are considering yourself as the body or the 'I' feeling as the body.

Alright. If you say that you never consider yourself as the body, then what you are? If you say that you are living in the body as a person lives in a house, you are not the body then and you must know how and where you are in the body. Ever you did consider in the whole of your body where from the feeling of 'I' is coming? How and what exactly it is? Why don't ever we consider about these important things? What is preventing us from doing that?

Because mind's nature is outwards. Just like when you pour water it moves downside, when awaken the mind just moves into the outside world. It does not know about anything else except the outside world and the material things it contains. As it is quite difficult to make the water upwards, making the mind move inwards as well is difficult. It is not impossible but difficult. But why it is difficult?

Just observe a small baby. It moves freely with the known people. It likes to spend most of the time with her mother. Why? Because from its birth it knows only those. In the same way from its birth mind knows only the world around and the material things in it. It does not know anything about the inside world. So it feels reluctant to move inside and to see the inside world.

What happens if we do leave our mind mingle and move with outside world so? What is the necessity to make it turn inside? However sweet and however good the material things around may appear, they don't last longer at all. The pleasure we do get by enjoying the material would not be in the same way all the time. We can enjoy sweat meats and other dishes while we are feeling hungry. We do relish them a lot while eating. But when you have become stomach full your attitude towards those dishes would change. After filling your stomach quite tight with the delicious dishes, you do get a vomiting feeling by looking at the same dishes which you have relished a lot while you were eating them. It is so almost with everything. The pleasure you do get by enjoying the material would not be the same all the time.

It is not just that, time passes unknowingly if you indulge yourself completely in enjoying the outside world and you become old and leave the body. After death it is indeed a blank wall. No one knows what happens afterwards. So it is not at all wise to use all our time only in enjoying the material available to us.

If you do want to escape from the cycle of birth and death what should you do? You have to become inwards. You must try to know what exactly you are. But how we can do that? Our mind does not have any knowledge about it. What would be the use in becoming inwards? What exactly becoming inwards means?

Inwards means withdrawing from the external. Our involvement in the outside world preventing us from going inwards. Our mind always tries to be in the outside world. It just cannot even think about there is something other than the material world.

In fact there is no necessity to do anything to go inside. If you can withdraw yourself from the outside automatically you can become inward. What all you need to do is reduce your indulgence in the outside world. However much great you may become, however much material you may enjoy, nothing remains after death. In fact it is the same thing whether you become so great a man or you remain so normal all your life it does not make any difference after death. If you remind yourself about this fact time and again automatically you get disinterest in the outside world and become inward.

The most surprising thing

What is the most surprising thing in the entire universe? It is not the solar planet, not the earth, not the seven wonders, not the technology we have got now. But what that would be then?

The feeling of 'I' in this body! Why it is in this body, where it has come from and where it goes when death comes to the body. Can you say when you really did feel the 'I' in your body for the first time? Surely it was not in the body when it has taken birth. Not even until third or fourth year. But then too only in a weak way. Not as strong as an elderly man feels it. Until it has become so strong, until the ego feeling starts in an unconquerable way, there is happiness and peace to us. But worries start, anxiety sprouts up, when this 'I' has taken full shape and clothed with ego. But what exactly this 'I' is? Why it has taken birth like this?

At this stage, at this point, it is indeed difficult to define it. It is really difficult to understand. But we do feel it only when there is mind. If there is no mind, there would be no feeling of 'I' either. In your deep sleep you are not feeling any mind and there is no feeling of 'I' either.

What we can deduce then? As both 'mind' and 'I' are existing or not existing? If they are true we have to be known and feel them at all times. What is happening to the 'I' along with the mind while we are in deep sleep? Where they are vanishing? Where from they come back and stick to us again when we wake up? If we do take the 'I' and the mind are just non-existing what we are without these? What all this world would be then? Whatever we are seeing around us, the aero-plane, television, computer, internet all this modern technology and several other things came as a thought in the mind first, before taking shapes like these. It can be clearly said without the mind none of these are in existence now. Therefore, you cannot simply strike of the existence of the mind just as an illusion or a vagary.

In the entire universe, mind is the most complex thing to understand. It is something that you never can say whether existing or not existing. Science never agrees with something that has not been made of atoms. For science, if it has not been made of atoms, it is not in existence at all. As the mind has not been made of atoms it just does not agree something like that existing. It is the great limitation of the science. It is not at all downgrading science. Science has its own greatness but it has its limitation like this.

But if we do want to know the true meaning of ourselves, winning over this mind is utmost important. If someone wants to win over his enemy what he would do? First of all he wants to know about the enemy's strong points and his weak points. Just blindly he would not try to face the enemy. If he does like that the chances of his being drubbed in his enemy's hands are more.

'Mind is a bundle of thoughts.' It has been said longtime back about the mind. But in my opinion mind is more than thoughts. Even there are no thoughts in your mind there will be feelings and imaginations. Every feeling and imagination need not be in a thought form in your mind. Even a small child which does not know any language feels happy when it sees its mother. So it can be safely said mind is a sack of feelings, imaginations and thoughts. If you can manage that there are no feelings, imaginations or thoughts in your mind you can make it nil and you do reach that super-conscious stage. But is it is possible? Can we do it like that?

Intentionally, with our own will it is an impossible task. Even it seems possible to you to prevent thoughts, feelings and imaginations in your mind by force it will be only for few minutes. After that all those invade into your mind with double force. Using force against the mind is a foolish task. We need to understand the nature of the mind before attempting to conquer it.

Try to think to what these thoughts, feelings or imaginations related to. They are mostly with regard to the things you have seen, enjoyed and experienced in the past. Sometimes the mind changes them in its imagination. For example you have seen a black crow in the past. Your mind can imagine a white crow.

For convenience sake mind can be divided into two parts. Conscious and subconscious. In fact only one mind does all this and the division is only for convenience. It can be said whatever you willfully and intentionally do is being done by your conscious brain. You have byhearted a poem and you did it with your conscious brain. You have made conversation with your friend and you did it with your conscious brain. So many things you do while you are awaken, you do them with your conscious brain. The point is your subconscious brain as well is in work while your conscious brain is working. While you are talking with your friend your subconscious brain observe some more features of him and store them carefully somewhere. While you are travelling in a train or bus or in your car thinking, your subconscious brain observes the nature around and some of that would be stored deep in your mind. When you have started at your home to go to your office in your car and fallen in deep thinking, that it is your subconscious brain makes you drive the car safely and reach the office.

Now we do think about 'I' and its relation with the body and the mind. With some difficulty, we can differentiate ourselves with the body. If you concentrate a few minutes, you can find out many important points. If you are the body itself why don't you know many things about it yourself? How did you come to know that hemoglobin is the reason for your blood being to be red? Someone did the research and told us. In the same way some other people did the research and said heart purifies the blood and pumps it throughout the body. Someone else did research and said that there are kidneys in your body and what they would do. The point here is, if you are the body itself, what is the necessity that someone else should say all these things to you? Why you are this much ignorant about it? Moreover why you are going to a doctor whenever your body gets illness? Why cannot you know about it yourself and treat yourself? In fact these are all the facts to prove substantively that you are not the body.

You may still think that the body is responding to your instructions. You think you are moving your hand as per your instructions. You are walking as per your instructions. Your body is behaving as per your instructions. How you can think that you are not the body?

Your body is your body only when your mind is associated with it. Your sensual organs are your sensual organs only when your mind associated with them. You can hear things only when your mind associated with your ear. 'I have called you many a time. You did not hear me at all.' after calling you many a time on your behind your friend has said to you. What that means? That does not mean you suddenly became deaf. That means your mind is not associated with your ears then. It is thinking about something else seriously so it is not with the ears. Therefore you could not hear your friend's calling.

'Why cannot you see me even I am before your eyes?' your wife said to you. She felt surprise as you did not notice her even she stood before your wide open eyes. That does not mean you have become blind. That means your mind not associated with your eyes. So, you do feel the body when the mind associated with it. Yours sensual organs do work only when your mind associated with them.

Mind, the great mediator, is between you and the body. In fact there is not that much difference between you and the mind as between you and the body. Differentiating yourself with the mind at this stage is only for convenience sake. Mind is like smell from a flower. Light from a bulb. Mind is just like a curtain between you and the real you. It is all appear typical and difficult to understand. Just try to think what there is if there are no feelings or thoughts. Can you say there is nothing? Just because of non-existence of the mind which is nothing but a bundle of thoughts and feelings as we discussed earlier, you too do become non-existent? Are you going to agree with this theorem?

If you do take it like this what about the deep sleep state? There is no mind at all to you then. Would you conclude that you do not exist in your deep sleep since you are having no sort of feeling then? It can be proved that you do exist while you are in deep sleep as much as you do exist in your awakened state. How you do feel when you are disturbed and wake up while you are in deep sleep? So much irritated. That you don't want to come out of that state at all. If possible you want to be in that state all your life. But why? There is no 'I' feeling in that state. You just don't have any knowledge whatsoever about where you are and what you are. Still why do you like that state?

Because it is not a nil state as you are thinking. Your mind merged with the real you. It is the total you then present. But it is indeed difficult to take mind as nothing. We cannot separate ourselves from the mind as we can separate ourselves from the body. It is only the mind that can experience something, think something and feel something. If you are feeling anything that is only with the mind. Other than mind what else there is? It is not comfortable to think that mind is completely perishable and separate from us.

Take a man at his five years age. How he would be at that stage? So innocent without any ego. He plays with dolls and laughs at all people who look at him. His knowledge level is so limited Consider the same man at his fifty years of age. How he would be then comparing with his five years age personality? So matured and so knowledgeable. He would not play with anything with which he played at his fifth year. The point here we need to consider is nothing destroyed. The same five years aged boy turned into a fifty years aged man with the passage of time. The same psyche in that small boy gradually evolved, elevated and matured and took a completely different dimension by the time he reached fifty.

In the same way it is the same mind that evolves into super consciousness. With dispassion and practice, mind can be elevated to the stage of super consciousness. Mind is not being destroyed but elevated to the highest and supreme level.

But one thing most of the saints are saying. Keep your mind still. The great saint Adi Sankara also said the same thing. 'Make your mind stand still. That is what called as salvation.' What a simple solution offered! To think it is something so simple. But in practice it is the most difficult thing.

You may say that in deep sleep there is no mind at all. It is happening so easily then. But one point you need to understand is it is happening without your intention. Quite automatically. Just try to make your mind still as it is in deep sleep while you are awaken. You can easily understand the difficulty in it.

We already have discussed about the mind. It is nothing but a bundle of thoughts, feelings and imaginations. For convenience sake we do consider thoughts, feelings and imaginations with a single word 'thought'. What is there if there are no thoughts? What would be left if all the thoughts vanish? To know about that we have to make the thoughts vanish first. It is something that can be experienced but cannot be told in words. Why it cannot be expressed in words? Because it is something that you do experience when your mind completely subdued. It is beyond your mind, your psychological state. So you can enjoy it, experience it but you cannot explain it in words. Explaining is something that you do your with your mind. This super consciousness is something beyond your conscious and subconscious minds.

Now we shall come to the main task 'make the mind free of thoughts.' All the meditational practices main purpose is make the mind free of thoughts. There are so many ways. We cannot say one way is better than the other. Every way has its own pros and cons. We have to choose the best way that suits to our mindset, our daily routine. Some of the prominent meditational ways are saying a mantra with concentration, chanting some Gods name, soundfulness, etc. If we practice one of the ways without getting discouraged, frustrated sure we do get what we have aimed at. Srikrishna said in Bhagavadgita 'practice and dispassion are the main tools to get that super consciousness.'

'Keeping the thoughts away by way of force' is not an advisable thing. With however much force you use to keep the thoughts away, thoughts do become that much powerful and haunt you down.

Think about the thinker

It is a strange thing to think or consider about the thinker and thoughts. Who is the thinker here and why do we think about him? We do have tons of thoughts everyday. The surprising thing is that we don't even know some of the thoughts while they are taking the whirlwind tour of our mind. We get irritated, frustrated but just don't know how to stop them. Anyhow the present task in our hand is to think about the thinker.

Before we consider the worth of the statement think about the thinker, we shall see whether there is a thinker or not. Why should there be a thinker in the first place? Why we are presuming that there is a thinker? Well, there are thoughts. So, there should be a thinker. How thoughts are possible without a thinker? Can thoughts come from nothing?

Some great philosophers say that there are only thoughts but no thinker. It is indeed difficult to think like that. If there is no thinker at all who that is observing the thoughts? Who that is saying I am having this thought? Who that is being influenced by the thought and becoming happy or sad by it?

In my opinion it is impossible to think that there is no thinker but only the thoughts. It is possible that there is thinker remains without thoughts but thoughts without thinker? Just unthinkable. Now we shall see how it is possible the thinker remains without the thoughts.

Everyday we quite usually do go through three states. Waking, dream and deep sleep. There shall be thoughts in waking and dream states. It is the unconscious thoughts appear like dreams to us. But in deep sleep where these thoughts are? What is really present while we are in deep sleep? This deep sleep state is indeed a great boon to mankind. It has been awarded to us only to understand what we exactly are. I often say to think about deep sleep. Deep sleep is the positive proof to us that it is possible to us to remain without worries, without anxieties. The most important point here is there is no 'I' feeling either in this deep sleep.

As many people do consider, deep sleep is not just inactive or slumber state. It is the most active, useful state to us. Then why do we never worry or think about it? Because it happens so easily and so naturally to us. If something comes to us without effort, without any work on our part we don't think that is something worthwhile. Deep sleep is something like that.

Don't think I am digressing. I am in the subject. We are considering about the possibility of the thinker remaining without thoughts. Do you say you are not in existence at all as there are no thoughts or no 'I' feeling in the body while you are in deep sleep? Is it is only the moss of body in existence while you are in deep sleep? Not at all. It is your real you that is in existence while you are in deep sleep. By this you must agree that there is a possibility of thinker remains without thoughts at all.

Now we shall think about this 'I'. What exactly it is? Bhagavan Ramana Maharshi said this 'I' feeling is nothing but a thought. This 'I' feeling comes before all the thoughts and it is the predominant thought. If we start inquiring about this 'I' thought, it disappears along with all the other thoughts. I agree. There is no 'I' at all and it is just mere a thought. But to whom to this 'I' thought and all the other thoughts are happening?

We cannot deny something that is quite similar to 'I' is in existence. It is quite impossible to think that there is nothing. If you do start thinking about this, you eventually come to the opinion that there should be a base to all this. A base that does not have another base but a base to all the other things. That base has no boundaries that base does not made of items. That base does not need eyes to see, ears to hear and other organs to function but it gives the power to all our organs to function. That base is this real 'I'.

That is what in existence while you are in deep sleep. If there is nothing in existence while you are in deep sleep, why do you feel so good and want it to continue like that? Why do you get irritated if someone disturbed you while you are in deep sleep? Because, that is your real state.

Now we shall think about our mind. It is the most complicated and surprising thing in the entire universe. Its existence itself is in question since it cannot be said whether it is really there or not. But there is nothing to us if mind is not there. Before we go too deep into this matter, we shall see what exactly this mind is.

As per the famous saying mind is nothing but a bundle of thoughts (Here we have to take imaginations, feelings also under thoughts). If there are no thoughts, there is no mind also. If there is no mind, what lies there? If you can manage to make that there are no thoughts, that there is no mind, your real you comes out. But is it is something easy to do? Can we make that there are no thoughts in our minds atleast for few minutes?

It is impossible to make ourselves free of thoughts at will. If we do try too hard, we may make ourselves free of thoughts at maximum half a minute. It is in fact suppression of thoughts and the thoughts do see all the time to jump into us again. In that half a minute or so thought free session also, we cannot feel any comfort. It would be a sort of uneasiness.

Before we worry about how to make ourselves completely free of thoughts, first we think why should we become free of thoughts? Thoughts are harmless and innocent. They cannot get any loss to you. Should we have to get rid of thoughts if we want complete peace?

There is no need to get rid of thoughts from our mind at all. Once we stop worrying about thoughts, or stop being influenced by thoughts, thoughts cannot do any harm to us. If we become neutral towards thoughts, that is, stop considering thoughts that do come into our mind, there is no difference whether there are thoughts or not in us. There is very interesting thing to consider about here.

Most people think thoughts plays an important role in our minds. In fact it is not so. It is the feelings that do play a very important role. Most of the thoughts do create feelings either happy or sorrow depend upon the nature of the thoughts. At the same time that there is no necessity that every thought does create a feeling. A thought about next elections may not evoke any feeling in you. The thought regarding the praise by your boss on yesterday evening does create a good feeling. The thought regarding the quarrel between you and your wife two days back creates a sad feeling. Thoughts that do not create either happiness or sorrow are called as neutral thoughts. At the same time that there is no necessity that every feeling should be evoked by a thought. Feelings can be there without being preceded by a thought. A month' aged baby cannot have any thoughts. But it sure does have feelings. A crying month aged baby stops that and smile happily when its mother took it into her hands. What causes the smile on the lips of the baby here? It is the feeling of inner happiness to it. Here it proves that feelings can be there without thoughts.

But the point is, if you can control the thoughts, you can control the feelings. If you do see that only good thoughts come into your mind all the time you do get only good feelings. By cultivating only good feelings you can change your whole life. It is a hard exercise in fact but it is also possible with constant practice.

But particularly trying to pull good thoughts into your mind is a tedious exercise and sometimes it creates headaches to you. Rather than that leave the thoughts without disturbing them and without even observing them irrespective the point whether they are positive or negative thoughts, good or bad thoughts. Just put yourself in the work you are doing without bothering about the thoughts. If you do practice it you can enjoy lot of peace.

Don't try to be perfect. Just try to be the best

Whatever you may be doing just don't try to make it hundred percent error free or mistake free but just try to make it the best. There is lot of difference between the 'perfect' and the 'best'. You have to apply your mind and put effort to do something perfectly. But to make something best you have to put your heart. I shall tell you what happens if we try to make something hundred percent perfect.

I used to type fast and good. There are only four or five mistakes in the matter I typed in the required time. My typing tutor also praised me a lot as I am doing typing with that much few mistakes. I too felt so happy and then I got an idea. How it would be if I try to do that typing without any mistake at all in that required time? I launched on that myself and tried to be so. Can you guess what happens? I did that typing with not less than twenty mistakes! Why it happened like that? Just because I have tried to make it perfect. When I typed without bothering for perfection, I put only my heart on that and there was no calculation or result orientation at all. I just want to make that best and I could. But when I tried to make that perfect and put my mind on it, it was spoiled like that.

I don't say result is not important but don't try to be result oriented. Leave the result to God and just try to do the thing in the best way possible. Put your heart in whatever you are doing instead of your mind and calculate only when it is necessary. It surely shall be so much helpful to you.

Get rid of the 'I' feeling. It gives you lot of peace and happiness

It was a place and there were some people assembled. All they were so happy and they were discussing something in themselves. Suddenly there came a person and huge boulder was on his head. It was so heavy and he was struggling very hard to keep it like that on his head.

"Why you are struggling yourself like that with the boulder? Throw it away." one of the people assembled there advised him.

"How it would be? This boulder is on my head from the moment I have got knowledge. It is my very identity. Without this boulder there is no identity to me at all." Breathing hard that person who was bearing that boulder on his head said.

"You are mistaken. There used to be boulders like that on our heads also. We all threw our boulders away and happy like this. You too may please just do it like that. You too can have the same happiness as we are all having." Another person in that assemblage said.

"I just cannot do it myself." That person wailed. "This boulder is very heavy and I cannot bear it. But I cannot throw it away myself. Please one of you does that for me." He pleaded.

"None of us can do that except yourself. We have thrown our boulders ourselves away. You too can throw your boulder away if you try. Just try to throw it away, it is possible." The same person advised him.

Then the person who was bearing the boulder on his head tried to throw the boulder away and surprisingly he could. After getting rid of that boulder he felt so light and his heart filled with utmost happiness.

Then he exclaimed "Thank God! Why did not I have got this idea before?"

The 'I' feeling in all of us is the boulder in fact. It makes us suffer like anything. Whatever we may do, we do it for that 'I'. We always think 'I' have to be praised, 'I' have to be glorified and 'I' never be criticized. Just forget about the rest in the sentence and think about the 'I'. Who it is? It is the boulder, it is the rock we are unnecessarily bearing in ourselves and suffering hell. Whoever gets rid of this 'I', this boulder, they do feel so happy. Whatever you may do, just try not to aim at the 'I'. Just do the work for work's sake. It appears foolishness, it appears difficult and painful but it is never so. It is most result yielding and happy thing in the entire universe.

Just try to observe the feeling you are having

It is some sort of meditation in fact. But the easiness and difference in this comparing with the meditation is it can be practiced anywhere either opening your eyes or closing them. It would be more useful to you while you are feeling sorrow, irritating, angry to get a hold on those feelings.

Take one or two deep breaths, close your eyes tightly and open them again. Then ask in yourself what I am feeling in myself now? Just try to acknowledge the feeling you are having at that time. It may be fear, anger, disgust or something like that. Soon you can have the feeling in your focus. Then just hold your concentration on that. Slowly you do get a feeling that you are having control over the situation. Why and how it has become possible like that? Just because, while doing like this, you have separated yourself from your mind. You are seeing, whatever feeling you are having at that time, separate and different from you. Once we see something separate from us, it would become easy to deal with it. If someone puts a lemon on your head, you cannot see it at all. If the same lemon has been put before your eyes it is easier to see and deal with. If you have become the feeling itself, you cannot deal with it at all. If you have separated yourself from the feeling, it would be so easy to deal with it.

Just like all the meditational practices, this also needs some practice. Don't get frustration if you cannot get the required result at the first instance itself. If you persist, you sure do get the result.

Everything depends how you do look at it

There are people who commit suicide even for silly and simple things also. There are people whose strong resolve make them stand firm even against the greatest difficulties. It just depends how we do take things around us. One person may take something so ghastly, unbearable and terrifying while the other person takes it so simple, easy to deal with.

Some people may feel fear even to take a small loan while the other people take huge loans and live happily. I am not either against or in favour of taking loans or not taking loans. I am just saying it as an example how people minds be influenced by their different tendencies of considering things.

Some people do take very seriously and get offensive if someone criticizes or curse them. Some other people take these types of incidents easily and forget them fast. My opinion is not to tolerate abuse and remain calm. If someone criticizes don't feel too much for it. Deal with it in the best way possible and forget about it

Some people do become very much upset with the disturbances in the families. With the revolutionary changes around, individual thinking and idiosyncrasies have become a norm among the family members also. If someone's daughter or son marries against his wish and will, he becomes too much upset for that. There are people who do take these types of things easily and let their sons or daughters with their lives with the partners they choose. Better we compromise ourselves with the things we cannot change rather than fighting with them tooth and neil.

Co-operation with the mind

There was a person named Mukund who was intelligent and educated. Once he became twenty five years or so aged his relatives thought that it would be better get him married. They found a girl Malathi and got his marriage performed with her. Mukund thought his life would be more and more happier if he married her and agreed to that marriage.

But the real problem started to Mukund only after the marriage. That girl Malathi was not wise at all. Her desires and wishes are quite foolish and disgusting. Moreover she was persistent and don't let Mukund go on with his life until he fulfils her desires. Mukund was becoming more and more frustrated and irritated on all of this.

He told everything to one of his relatives who played an important part in performing his marriage with Malathi "I cannot manage to live with her anymore. I want to get rid of her."

"It is not as easy as to marry her. You cannot get rid of her that easily at all." That person smiled and said.

"But how.....her wishes and desires are so foolish and disgusting....."

"Just see...." the other person interrupted Mukund and said. "This girl Malathi is not as much educated as you are. She is not an intelligent girl either. The perceptive ability of her mind and her knowledge about the world around are not that much. But......" he stopped for a moment and said. "If you understand her a little, if you cooperate with her a little, she shall be so much helpful to you. She cleans your clothes, cooks your food and does lot of work. In the absence of her, you yourself need to do all this work. Just try cooperate with her and fulfill some of her disgusting wishes and you can have her complete cooperation."

Mukund did just like that and very soon Malathi has become so malleable to him and so cooperative with him and his life has a drastic positive change.

Here Mukund is you and Malathi is your mind. Your mind does not have the level of your perception, level of your intelligence and it is born out of the world around. Sometimes its wishes and desires would be quite disgusting and irritating. But if you help it in fulfilling some of its wishes and desires however much disgusting and be tolerated with it, it shall be quite helpful to you.

Nothing above mentioned is impossible to practice and achieve. It all needs patience. If you patiently practice it it sure does give you the result. I am saying this with experience. Only after I have got the positive result I narrated the above techniques. Thank you very much for your interest in my book. If you leave a review I shall be even more grateful to you.

The End

Don't miss out!

Visit the website below and you can sign up to receive emails whenever Kotra Siva Rama Krishna publishes a new book. There's no charge and no obligation.

https://books2read.com/r/B-A-ATOV-ABOTC

BOOKS 2 READ

Connecting independent readers to independent writers.

Did you love *Body, Mind and You*? Then you should read *English Grammar Simplifier*[1] by Kotra Siva Rama Krishna!

This English grammar book was written keeping in view particularly all those who want to get a grip on English grammar. This book sure does give an understanding of English grammar and especially quite helpful to those who started learning English language. A systematic reading of this English grammar book will be immensely helpful to all those who want to gain command over English grammar.

---

1. https://books2read.com/u/mgPzEq

2. https://books2read.com/u/mgPzEq

Also by Kotra Siva Rama Krishna

Two Strangers On The Bed
A Girl's Conflict
Enna
Strawberry
Dusk
Just Relax!
Delicious Predicament
Nirupama
Half Opened Doors
Lovenest
Moonshine
Scarecrow
Closed Doors
Disturbed
Handfuls of Sand
Mansion of Illusions
Rain Flower
Rose Garden
Sand Dunes
Snow Flower
Split Personality
Being Possessed
Objection Sustained
House of Delusions
Rustle in the Leaves

Sasikala
Amaswitha
English Grammar Simplifier
Wisps of Smoke
Shadow in the Mirror
Love is Dangerous with a Stranger
Shadow of a Spirit
Unwanted Guests
Broken Window
Loud Thunder Nearby
Spirit in the Mirror
Whispers in the Night
Shadows in the Twilight
Twisted Shadow
Body, Mind and You
Summer Holidays
Flower of the Mist
Nail Polish
Laughter of a Spirit
Lipstick